HOW
WHEN YOUR FAMILY'S
CRACKING UP!

HOW TO STAY **SANE** WHEN YOUR FAMILY'S CRACKING UP!

COLIN PIPER   CHRIS CURTIS   TIM DOBSON

Scripture Union
130 City Road, London EC1V 2NJ

Cover design by Julian Smith
Artwork by Matt Gill

© Colin Piper, Christopher Curtis, Tim Dobson 1993

First published 1993

British Library Cataloguing-in-Publication Data.
A catalogue record for this book is available from the
British Library.

ISBN 0 86201 854 4

Phototypeset by Intype Ltd, London.

Printed and bound in Great Britain by Cox & Wyman
Ltd, Reading, Berkshire

Contents

1 Introduction

She was crying. . . She had found a picture of a woman
in dad's wallet and it wasn't her!

It was an ordinary school day, just like any other really, and I was just about to leave for school when I remembered I had forgotten something. I turned around and went back into the front room where I had just left my mother. She was crying. This really distressed me and I asked what was wrong. She gave me the usual 'nothing, go to school!' but I pestered on until she told me. She had found a picture of a woman in dad's wallet and it wasn't her! What could we do?

Suddenly and dramatically Steven's life had fallen apart. The family he had known and grown up in for sixteen years was finished. His father whom he loved and trusted had deceived him, and his mother whom he loved felt broken. All kinds of emotions swept through him. His head spun with bewilderment and disbelief at all that had suddenly happened. He was confused.

How did he feel towards his dad? Up to then there had been love. Now cutting through that love was anger and hurt for what dad had done to mum, him and his brothers. He felt guilty about these feelings. Only minutes before he had loved his dad but now. . .

Then there was mum. The mum who as a child he had run to and been comforted by. Now here she was, crying on and clinging to him. He hated her tears. He hated his dad who had caused them. He hated himself because he couldn't stop them. Did he even hate her for making him so helpless? He felt frustrated and drained. He felt useless.

Soon other thoughts began to flood his stunned mind. What would they do? Would they have to leave their home? How would his younger brothers react? Who could he turn to? Who should he tell? Should he tell anyone? Perhaps it would all be sorted out and could return to normal and then no one would need know? But what if it didn't? Where were they going to get money from? What normally happens in a situation like this? He didn't have a clue. Why, oh why, did God let this happen?

Over the coming months Steven was to live from crisis to crisis. There was to be little relaxation at home. He wanted to get out. But now mum depended totally on him. He was to face the horror of meeting the woman whose picture his mother had found in his dad's wallet. He was to be caught up in the solicitors' letters over home, money, even screwdrivers!

This is just one story repeated in thousands of homes every day across Britain. Each one differs.

Steven's life had fallen apart.

For some young people the breakup of the family isn't a shock but a gradual and painful process. For some it is a relief. Some feel trapped and unable to cope with it all. Others feel hurt and frustrated that their parents won't tell them what is going on. Others are just scared their family is falling apart and they feel helpless to stop it. This book has been put together with the help of teenagers, most of them Christians, who have gone through their own family nightmares, in order to help other young people through theirs.

2 The perfect family!

I had a bad car crash . . .

It was great being in my family. It was somewhere I always felt at home, safe and secure. We had a routine that ran so smoothly, and we all got on so well.

I was really proud of my mum. Everyone liked her. She was a brilliant cook and kept the house looking amazing. She had this knack of knowing just when you needed someone to talk to and always had time to spare. Even though there were four kids in our family she made each one of us feel special and we all thought we were her favourite.

Dad had a busy job but we weren't last on his list of priorities. After tea each night would be his time with us as a family. He would help mend my bike or else play games with us. The things he used to show us or teach us were brilliant. And on our family holidays we used to have such a wild time. He has a wicked sense of humour. But the thing I liked best were the times we used to spend alone together. We didn't say much, we would just sit there. In the quiet I knew that he really loved me and cared a lot.

It's funny how in a time of crisis we pulled together. Like when I had a bad car crash with my mum and brother. We were trapped in the wrecked car for about half an hour but to be able to talk to mum, and I suppose most of all to talk to God, was so reassuring. Even when mum was in hospital for a couple of months we pulled together and became closer still.

Another fight with my older brother. Another shouting match with dad and constant nagging from mum. My sister has borrowed my favourite sweatshirt and has left it dirty and screwed up in the corner of my bedroom.

Why do I have to be part of a family?

Why THIS family?

Why couldn't I be a frog?

Miss Smith in 8th year Biology said that after the frogs eggs have been fertilised they're left to grow without interference from their parents! Sounds great to me!

God's intention for family

When God thought up the idea of family couldn't he see how things would go so badly wrong?

God must have reasons for putting us in families and wanting us to stay in them. So before looking at the problems of family breakdown it's important to get an idea of what God's initial plan for family was.

As we all have different experiences of family life let's look to see what the Bible says about it all.

The first place family is mentioned is right at the start of the Bible in Genesis. Just after God created Eve, the first woman, it says, 'For this reason a man will leave his father and mother [family] and be united with his wife [to become another family]'.

Through the Old Testament we see countless stories of different families. There are tragedies like the first family breakdown where Cain killed his brother Abel. And there are triumphs when God miraculously provided a son for the old, childless couple, Abraham and Sarah. We see the tensions of a family with divided loyalties when mother and son (Rebecca and Jacob) plot to deceive dad (Isaac). And there are trials of favouritism between Joseph and his brothers.

Throughout the whole of the Old Testament a great emphasis is put on family. But why? I think that there are two main reasons why God made us different from frogs.

1 To provide a loving, positive and secure environment where children grow, develop and learn to live and love.

2 To provide a picture through our parents of what God is like.

Let's take a closer look at each of these reasons.

1. Family as God intended

From the very start God wanted to share his love with others. So he made us. His plan was that we should be like him and in turn share his love with others. He hoped that one day we would become just like Jesus (conformed to the image of his Son, is the way the Bible puts it). God thought that family was the best context for this to start to happen.

Believe it or not God really intended family to be a place where we could first experience what it was like to be loved and cared for: as Mum and Dad smiled and 'gooed' at us, fed us and changed our nappies! He intended it to be a place where we could grow and learn basic skills like eating, walking and talking in a secure, stable setting. Family was to be where we learned what it meant to be committed to other people and to help and serve each other. Does this sound incredible! Let me explain a bit more.

Belonging

I remember well the day my younger sister got stuck in the lift at the multi-storey car park. Clutching a cage of baby mice that were prone to escape at any time, she rushed into the lift as soon as the doors opened. Before we had time to follow, the doors had closed and the lift was off. Someone with a wicked sense of humour had decided that it should go to the twelfth

I remember well the day my younger sister got stuck in the lift . . .

floor. Rushing up the stairs we managed to keep pace with the lift. We waited at each floor in vain for the lift to stop. Instead we heard only the tearful wailing of my sister getting louder as the lift approached, and fading away above. I thought it was hilarious. Mum was more concerned. When the lift finally did stop on the top of the car park, my sister rushed out into mum's arms with a final sob.

We never did find the mice.

I don't know if you can remember as a child ever getting lost in a big supermarket or in a car park. But I expect you can imagine what it must feel like, being alone and frightened. What a sense of relief when eventually you find mum or dad and you dash towards them. Everything suddenly seems to be OK. In their arms or holding their hand, we feel safe and secure.

We all need to feel we belong somewhere or to someone and that is why God put us in families. That is where we belong. That is where we should feel 'at home' and relaxed – where we should feel secure as we face a sometimes hostile world around us. Even if people stop being our friends, in our family mum and dad will always be our parents and we will always be their child.

Growing

When you plant seeds in the garden, aside from green fingers, you need the right conditions – good soil, enough water, plenty of sunshine and warmth (and for some of us a bit of luck!). In the same way children need the right conditions to grow healthily. And this is where family comes in. That doesn't just mean physically, by mum giving you the right food, making sure you eat your greens (and not too many sweets!). It means helping us to grow emotionally, mentally and spiritually too! As parents spend time with their children caring for them and playing games, a child's emotions like laughter, love, patience, trust and respect begin to develop. As a family gets a chance to sing and pray together, and read about Jesus, a child will grow spiritually too.

Learning

The growl came from the bathroom. It was uncannily like mum's warm up sounds of annoyance as she worked herself up to tell off her eighteen-month-old daughter. But this was not mum. She was standing next to me in the kitchen. It could only have been one person, our darling daughter herself. What followed confirmed this in a most embarrassing way. As we looked stunned at each other the final rebuke echoed from the bathroom through the hall and into the kitchen. 'You naughty dolly . . . shut your face!' Where had she learnt that phrase?

We all like to copy or mimic others. You can see it sometimes in a child who copies their father or mother (mostly bad habits I hasten to add!). The family should be a great place for learning. From the earliest years we learn by following the example given to us by mum or dad. How to talk, how to eat or how to tidy up (or leave a room untidy). God also intended parents to teach or train their children not just by example but by words as well.

How many times have you been punished, grounded or disciplined in some way? Loads I expect! Discipline in the family helps us to learn what is right and wrong, what is acceptable behaviour and what is not. We inevitably get punished when we constantly disobey instructions or get shouted at when, for instance, we go too near a fire. But through all these things we can learn valuable lessons that help us enjoy life and live safely.

2. Family shows us what God is like

The second reason that God put us in families was to try to show us something of what he is like. This might be hard to understand, particularly as so many families seem to go wrong. But when we start to get it together then we get a brilliant picture of what God and his love is like.

Pictures help us understand what God is like. The Bible says he is like a rock or he is like a fortress and an eagle. Now we know that God is not literally a Cosmic Rock, a Mega Fortress or a Divine Eagle but they are all pictures showing us something of his character.

God also uses the picture of a mother and a father. So the Bible says things like:

'Can a mother forget the baby at her breast and have no compassion on the child she has borne? [The answer should be "No".] Though she may forget, I will not forget you!'

'As a mother comforts her child so will I comfort you.'

'God carried you as a father carries a son.'

'As a father has compassion on his children, so the Lord has compassion on those who fear him.'

So families should help us learn about God. As our earthly father should care for us, protect us and provide for us, we learn from his 'living picture' that God as a heavenly father can do the same. As our earthly mothers should feed us, comfort us when hurt and listen to our problems so God in heaven will 'feed' us, comfort us and listen to us, as a perfect mother. How amazing and what a challenge it is, that parents can actually show their children by their lives what God is like.

3 The disappearing family

The bombshell of a family breakdown hits in many different ways.

The blow across the head awoke Sir Roderick with a start. He glanced around him, assessed the situation and shut his eyes again. He pieced together the facts as he saw them. The object that had hit him was a small paperback book, now lying to his right on that bit of carpet that still smelt of . . . well to keep to the point, on his right. The aggressor must have been Master John, partly because he had been reading the book as he, Sir Roderick, had dropped off and partly because he now had a rather apologetic smirk on his face.

In his typical forgiving way Sir Roderick said nothing. He simply went back to sleep again. This was his normal way of dealing with crisis. Well that, or a short stroll round the garden. You see by nature Sir Roderick was a very placid dog. More than that he was very understanding: well, as Golden Retrievers go anyway. He knew John had lost his sense of humour recently. He didn't just mean that John now objected to being ambushed whilst walking down the path. (Him and his fancy street cred gear!) More understandably the situation at home was getting to him. It was even getting to the placid, some would say just plain slobby, Sir Roderick.

John grunted an apology to poor old Sir Roderick. *But that book!* he thought. *That wretched book! Who ever wrote that last chapter should come and live at 8 Beaconsfield Road. They would then find out what a real family is like. Mum and dad arm in arm gazing lovingly at their obedient, adoring children! Not here! Mum or dad in an arm lock perhaps. That I can imagine. But us kids don't hang around long enough to find out. This place is depressing, even scary.*

It all began to go wrong. Do you know I can't

*remember where it began to go wrong? And why?
Why can't mum love dad again? I want a happy family
like before! But were we ever happy? I don't know. I'm
getting depressed again. I am not going to cry. I
haven't so far and I'm not now. But why us? Why?
Why? Why?*

As the tear began to roll down John's face, Sir
Roderick started the movement to roll over onto his
back. He was a master of the emotions of the moment.
He felt the tension of hurt and knew how to bring relief.
At that moment John stared down through glazed eyes
at the ridiculous sight of the noble Sir Roderick with
four legs in the air and his tail arched up to cover his
private parts. He couldn't help himself. He laughed.
'Come on, lets go for a walk,' he said, getting up. He
looked down and laughed again. 'I wish I was like you.
You haven't a clue have you?'

Sir Roderick grinned stupidly and growled know-
ingly.

Finding out what went wrong

I was sitting in the garden reading. It was hot. I had
finished my exams. Life was good. Dad came and sat
next to me. Funny he was home so early. We talked.
Not a lot. Most of the time there was silence. It didn't
occur to me he was building up to say something. But
then he said it – I'm leaving home. It was a total shock.
I was stunned. My head suddenly filled with questions
but the main one was 'Why?' It was unreal, like some
bad joke come true.

The bombshell of a family breakdown hits in many
different ways. It may be one big instantaneous

17

explosion. It may be a blitz that builds up and goes on for years before the inevitable happens. But however it comes, one question always echoes through the despair, anger and hurt: Why?

Working out what went wrong is sometimes easy but at other times can be very hard indeed. It is often even harder to work out who is to blame, especially if, like in one of those infuriating Agatha Christie novels, you aren't given all the facts. You will though want to know what has gone wrong and why. If you aren't told the reason or if it isn't obvious, your imagination is likely to invent one.

This is particularly true of younger children who can't understand what is going on. They accept the only explanation their conscience in all its bewilderment, ignorance and despair can concoct: 'It's my fault.' Over the years this theory becomes engrained as truth and the facts changed accordingly to fit in with it.

Even when older and more able to understand the true strains marriages undergo, lack of information and explanation from mum or dad leave all reasoning to your imagination. Your mind in its emotional state turns the sensational into the plausible and finds you guilty of causing the problems. We shall see later that many young people grow up wondering whether their family failed because of them. But ninety-nine times out of one hundred this is just not true.

Talking about what went wrong
Most likely, the cause of the breakup of your family lies with mum or dad or both. It is important therefore that you should ask mum and dad

to tell you what has gone wrong. They may not want to do so. They may find it hard to talk about personal things with you anyway. They may still see you as their little child and think you wouldn't understand. They may not understand themselves what has gone wrong. They may not want you to know of the failings of their partner. They may feel it could hurt you or may sort itself out and life would more easily return to normal with you in the dark.

It is so useful to talk about the problems. My experience is that most mums and dads never realise their children could somehow blame themselves for wrecking the family. Then again a mum or a dad who is doing all they can in the situation to be a good parent, can feel guilty about letting you down. Talking will help put the record straight. It might even make it clearer what has gone wrong and what might help put things right. It certainly can bring you closer.

Believing what went wrong

Even when we are told or know of our mum and dad's faults it is still sometimes hard to believe them. As a child you may have boasted of your dad's superhuman abilities. As the boasting reaches a climax your dad evolves into a cross between Rambo, Einstein and the Governor of the Bank of England. As you grow older he seems to lose his touch a little and his style totally. You try to keep him out of the sight of your friends at all costs in case he does, says or wears something embarrassing. But all the same it is hard to admit he could do something as hurtful as leave home or worse.

Unfortunately mums and dads can do hurtful things, and for many different reasons. If you want a rundown on some of these this next section is for you. You may though be only too aware of what's gone wrong in your family and want to know how to cope with it. If so, go on to the next chapter and I'll catch you up in a bit.

Understanding what went wrong

The immediate cause of your family breaking up might appear very obvious. For instance, the problem may be that mum has been drinking. But there may be stresses that lie behind the problem – worries at work. Then there are weaknesses that allow these stresses to get the better of her – more on that later.

The stress points

The final problems often are a result of various stresses that occur over a period of time. There are many of these.

Hardships such as debt, unemployment, cramped or shared living conditions and illness cause people to become depressed and difficult to live with. Alternatively they themselves might not be able to cope. Either mum or dad might find some escape in another relationship or else in drink. There might also be arguments. They might lose all confidence and just leave.

Responsibilities such as demanding jobs and families can wear mum and dad down and come between them. They may spend more time with others or just less time alone together. The resulting problems can be the same.

Change Over time we all change. Look at that old wedding photo on the sideboard. So much has changed. Apart from the hair styles (or the mere fact dad had hair) mum's looks have changed. They've got older. Not all people cope with this fact. In the same way as you found changes in your body as a young person disconcerting, some older people do too! We shall see later that if there are some weaknesses in mum or dad these changes can get the better of them. Other changes over time might include frustration and unfulfilment with their life. This produces restlessness; or general tiredness making them lethargic or boring. In fact we change in so many ways over the years that if a marriage is to survive it requires a tremendous commitment.

The problems
As we said before, these stresses can cause various problems that cause a marriage to break up. We can list the most common reasons given by people. Some face just one of these problems, others a number of them, a few face all of them.

Unfaithfulness Mum or dad has a relationship outside of the marriage. This may be sexual. It may not have got that far. You may see the other person involved as the major culprit behind all that's happened.

Arguments These may follow on from any of the other problems listed here or else be due to the other stress points we think about later.

Some face just one of these problems . . . a few face all
of them.

Alcohol and violence These often, though not
always, go together. Violence, as well as being
physical, can include verbal abuse and emotional
humiliation.

Inability to cope This can result from the other
partner's problems in one of the areas above or
the other stress points we talked about before.

The weaknesses
To survive, marriage has to be taken seriously.

1   You have to be sure you know really well the
person you are marrying.
2   You need to make a commitment to each other
which basically says I am simply going to love. It
doesn't matter what happens, I am going to love
you.

A marriage fails when we fail to do these two things. People can make a mistake in the first place because they were rushed or hurried into marriage too quickly or too young. We change so much between our late teens and mid twenties that early marriages are often under the most strain. Sadly people can be conned by others as well. Sometimes a mismatch is quickly obvious, with other marriages it may take time, and some of the stress points mentioned above, to highlight the problem. Either way it will necessitate an extra commitment of love by both mum and dad to make it work.

Unfortunately the real weakness, which prevents a marriage overcoming stress and resisting the problems, is when one partner doesn't in his or her heart stick to this commitment of love. When one of them allows selfishness into the marriage then weakness comes in too. If a man marries a woman for her looks, then when that marriage reaches the stress point of ageing the weakness is revealed. If the man then goes off looking for someone younger with new looks then there is a problem which is not easily worked out. Beneath the problems and the stress points of marriage often lies something as basic as selfishness.

This doesn't mean everyone who agrees to separate is selfish. There is a limit to how much you can go on loving in the face of rejection and abuse. True marriage is a two-way commitment. When this commitment is absent from one or both partners the marriage is weakened, even if it may soldier on for years before finally collapsing. The result of a good marriage is phenomenal love, the result of a collapsed marriage is heartbreak and hurt not just for the couple but for young people like you.

4 Inner space: You and your feelings

How do you get rid of, or at least come to terms with, these alien emotions?

25

Sir Roderick liked watching television. All those adverts for 'Whiskers'. It looked quite delicious. And it was certainly popular with nine out of ten owners. He knew that because John's mum often served it up for the rest of the family. 'Stewed Surprise' she called it. He couldn't understand why John and the others groaned.

John's mind was anywhere but on the TV screen. In fact he was staring at the framed picture on the sideboard next to it. Mum and dad smiled back at him. With arms around each other, their expressions told of happier times. Mum in her white wedding dress looked radiant and joyful; dad, in his flares and nylon jacket looked, well, embarrassing. He knew dad still had the jacket and wore it on odd occasions, much to the amusement of everyone else.

Dad! Why oh why had it gone wrong? John's thoughts began to rise in anger as he remembered all that had happened. He felt confused, even frightened. He loved his dad. He was his father after all. And yet he hated him for what he had done to his mum and his brother. He felt a tinge of guilt even as he thought of it. Could he, should he, hate his dad? Next to the picture was a model squirrel. He thought of the hours he and dad had spent in the loft carving and shaping it from a piece of wood. They had chatted for ages, had to be dragged down for meals, shared jokes together. All that seemed to have been thrown back in his face. Didn't it count for anything? How could his dad stop loving him after all they'd done together?

Sir Roderick, momentarily bored by the flashing pictures they seemed to put on between adverts, was also looking at the squirrel. It bothered him greatly. Whatever it was, it had managed to stand still for a very long time now. He was sure it moved from time to time. It used to be on the shelf for a start. The one time he had tried to scare it off by getting up there just to show it how big he was, John's mum had shrieked at him in horror. Didn't she understand he was just trying to protect them all?

The more John thought about what had happened, the more the emotions began to arise in him. He hardly ever cried. The day they threw his teddy out by mistake was an exception. But now tears began to roll down his cheeks. One by one they gathered pace as he struggled to come to terms with his feelings. If mum and dad were so happy before he came along, maybe he was partly to blame. Dad was always accusing mum for being too soft with them. And then there was the time he'd ruined mum's prize begonias when dad had sent him out to do the weeding. The flowers had been forgotten in the bitter argument that followed. And he'd started it, hadn't he?

By the time John's face had begun to resemble a water slide for ants, Sir Roderick had twigged that something was wrong. He had already sensed John's unhappiness for a few weeks but couldn't understand what John wanted him to do. Tears were different. He knew what to do with tears.

'Get off me you saliva maniac,' groaned John. He gave the dog a push towards the floor. This was even better, thought Sir Roderick. Master John wanted a tug of war too. He happily obliged by grabbing hold of the nearest convenient limb. It happened to be an arm.

'Alright.' John was laughing now. 'I get the message. Dinner time. But you ought to learn to ask nicely. You need some training you know.'

Training? It was a word that struck terror deep into

his heart. A subject he'd managed to avoid so far, and he had no intention of that changing. But it was a momentary thought, and soon Sir Roderick's mind was back where it belonged: on food.

Perhaps I'll be treated to 'Whiskers' for once, he thought, remembering the advert. It was clever the way they used cats in it just to get dogs' attention. John was in the kitchen by this time. He pulled a tin from the cupboard. 'There, how about a nice tin of Bonzo?'

Sir Roderick tried to smile.

Facing up to family breakdown is more than understanding what is going on at home. The biggest challenge for you may be what's going on in your head and heart. Feelings and emotions hit you like a ten ton truck, leaving you hurt and confused, even guilty.

'Best days of your life,' they tell you. 'No real responsibility. A chance to enjoy life before you become a boring adult!'

Some chance.

I've lost count of all the different feelings rushing round my head and heart. Sometimes just an image on the telly or the slightest comment set them off. My heart begins to pound. The guilt rises – anger, bitterness, fear, jealousy. Yes, I know, it seems incredible doesn't it? That I should feel jealous. But I do. I look at Susan, Sarah and the other girls talking about their latest family outing in their happy nuclear family and the feeling just comes. The only thing nuclear about my family is the bomb that hit us when dad left. We're still picking up the pieces.

How do you cope? Do you have a right to feel this way? Is it wrong to feel jealous that everyone else seems to have got a better family deal than you? You may never have been rejected by someone you love before. You may have never imagined you could feel anger and hate to this degree. Your guilt at harbouring these feelings only makes things worse. How do you get rid of, or at least come to terms with, these alien emotions? Help! !

A few years ago, Disney brought out a film called *Inner Space*. In it, a man is miniaturised and travels around another human body in a hi-tech pod.

Why on earth am I telling you this?

Well, for the next two chapters, I want to do the same thing. Injected into your body, we're going to travel to your heart and examine some of the feelings and emotions we find. One by one, let's work out why they're there and what to do about them. Ready? (What do you mean, you don't like injections? ?)

I feel rejected by mum and/or dad

When my parents used to have 'discussions' I was sent to my room where I could hear everything that was said. All I could do was cry. When my dad came in one day I ran over to kiss him. I noticed he was in a bad mood. Mum started speaking to him and he told me to 'buzz off!' I ran into my room and heard them shouting. What had I done wrong? Why was Daddy angry with me? As I heard them shouting, I felt like dying. I couldn't stick this anymore. I grabbed a part of my bedding, put some in my mouth and over my face. I wanted to die, to stop them fighting about me. After a while (I'm not sure how long) I took the bedding away from my face. A few minutes later the front door slammed and Mum went into the bedroom.

Psychologists tell us that the one thing we need and want more than anything else in life is not money or stardom but to be loved and accepted by other people. Their love gives a sense of value and purpose to our lives. We feel special, we feel we belong because the people around us accept and love us. The flip side of the coin is that the thing we struggle with and get hurt by the most in life is the opposite of being loved: being rejected. This is what hurt Julie when dad said 'buzz off'.

In fact, we go to extraordinary lengths to avoid rejection all the way through our lives. Wearing the right clothes – whether they're huge flares or tight drainpipes – doing the right things and listening to the right music are just examples of the way we make sure our friends at school won't reject us. Advertisers play on this fact to make us buy their products. We feel pressurised to 'fit in because we don't want to risk being laughed at and rejected by the people around us. For years I have kept my love of Abba's music secret for just that reason! The pressure to fit in is enormous.

That means when it does come, rejection hurts like nothing else. It scores a direct hit at your inner need for love and leaves you feeling wounded where it hurts most. Our sense of worth and value is challenged or even destroyed. In effect, people are saying 'You're not important. You're not valuable.'

What's more, as much as rejection by friends or boyfriends/girlfriends hurts, rejection by parents seems a million times worse. The very people you thought you could rely on, have left you. In effect, they seem to have said that their own happiness is more important than you. Your sense of value is crushed. Perhaps you imagine that others will do the same. An off-hand comment by a friend hurts, whereas before it would have been laughed off. How should you react to these feelings of rejection? Sally's dad left home when she was a little baby but her reaction was like many others:

I'm still afraid even now that as my dad didn't like me the way I am, no one else would.

How do I deal with rejection?

Well, first off, mum or dad leaving home may have not been rejection of you as their son or daughter. They may have already stayed together under increasing strain simply for you and your brother's and sister's benefit. When they do leave, the greatest problem for them may be the thought of leaving you. They may have decided that a separation, with an end to the arguments and tension, is in your best interests. They are rejecting the situation in which they find themselves, not you.

Sadly it is also possible that their motives are more selfish. By leaving home, they are deciding that their own happiness and fulfilment outweighs your need to have a home with both parents present. They may simply find it impossible to cope with the pressures and responsibilities of marriage and/or parenthood. But even then, they are not usually rejecting you outright. They still love you, even if that love is imperfect. They still want to be a parent to you, even if they are not at home.

Unfortunately, in some cases, mum or dad may be acting wholly selfishly. They may want to sever all connection with the family and pursue a new life, perhaps with a new partner. Coping with this is especially hard. Your friends and other family will need to support and love you more than ever before. Their love may not replace your mum or dad's love, but it will help you begin to build a sense of worth and value once again.

A Christian believes that our sense of worth as human beings does not derive from how much other people love or reject us. If that were so, we would be constantly vulnerable and constantly hurt. It comes from God, who made us with value and purpose and loves us with no strings attached. The value he places on every single one of us is extraordinary and beautiful. His intention was that it would be echoed and confirmed by your parents' love. In the absence of that, God's love does not change, as Sally was to find out:

It wasn't until I became a Christian just over a year ago that I realised that, although my father tossed me aside and didn't acknowledge my existence, God knows me, the actual me, and loves me for what I am, and that's really special to me.

I'm afraid of being alone

Finding yourself living with one parent can bring all kinds of new fears. Overnight the security of a family has been exchanged for a situation full of insecurities and uncertainties. One of these may be the fear of losing mum and being left completely alone. This fear may be increased if mum is or has been seriously ill.

If we give ourselves over to these fears it's difficult to know where to stop. You could live in constant fear of being run over by a car and refuse to go out of the house, you might never travel by air in case of an accident. In fact your whole life could be limited and dominated by fear. To try and live on such a basis would be ridiculous. Yes these things might possibly happen, but we can never be certain. All of us have to go through life with these uncertainties in the background, but we cannot let them dominate us.

When tragedy does strike, we are rarely completely alone. Brothers, sisters, relatives, neighbours, God, friends, church, social workers and council helpers are always there. Perhaps you may even enter into a relationship that begins to provide its own sense of security and may lead to marriage. All of these are possible and give us the support to deal with future problems.

I'm afraid that if I marry, the same thing will happen to me

When I was ten years old my family had a car accident in France. How we survived I'll never know. I was old enough to understand the seriousness of ambulances and oxygen masks; but unfortunately not old enough to be told what was going on. It made me even more afraid in the chaos. For many years after I was petrified of getting into a car. If we went over thirty miles-an-hour I broke into a cold sweat! The problem was this: I was afraid the same thing was going to happen again.

Witnessing the painful breakdown of mum and dad's marriage may encourage the same reaction in you. You may have watched the mistakes your parents have made and realised you are capable of the same. Alternatively, you might have watched mum and dad make a real attempt to patch things up and fail, and so you vow you will never marry. The risks of loving are too great. Like me, following my car accident, you're afraid. The alternative to marriage, living together, may suddenly become more attractive, enabling you to escape if things go wrong.

But wait a minute. Let's think about this for a moment. There's no logic behind the idea that 'if it's happened to them, it'll happen to me.' Millions of people have grown up in difficult family situations and gone on to have happy successful married lives. Nor will the option of living together protect you from being hurt. In some ways it could leave you more exposed without the sense of long-term commitment that marriage brings. Marriage encourages couples to seek an answer to their difficulties rather than give up. The easy option is not always the best one.

As impossible as it may seem, your experience may even have a beneficial effect on your future relationships. Your experience with mum and dad may have brought home to you the difficulties and challenges of marriage. You may be much more cautious about such a commitment, but that's no bad thing. Many young people never really understand these challenges and enter marriage on the thinnest of reasons, only to struggle later. If your experience has helped you comprehend this and brought about a wary caution, you will face life with an advantage over many of your friends.

I feel that it's my fault

At first I blamed myself because I thought they'd argued and split up over something I said.

I used to think I was a mistake – though I don't now – but I still feel I wasn't what my dad wanted. So he left partly because of me.

I wondered what I had done to make my dad stop loving me and my mum and my sister.

I used to think they were arguing about me and that I had done something wrong.

My mum wasn't meant to have children. She's totally career minded and only had us for our dad.

If one of these stories rings true, you, like many many others, may find yourself wondering if you are to blame in some way for what's happened. The old-fashioned wedding picture on the sideboard shows mum and dad in some outdated clothes smiling happily. It seems that before you came along they were blissfully happy. Perhaps your birth was a straining factor. Perhaps you were never wanted anyway. You were a mistake and although they did all they could, in the end you were just too much, too difficult and you broke them.

Alternatively you might wonder if you were the last desperate hope for mum and dad. The strain was already there before you were born, and you were to be the unifying factor. The wonder of creating a beautiful, new being was to bring a new shared purpose and delight into the relationship. Unfortunately, somehow you failed to do this. You were either awkward or just generally disappointing and consequently you brought an end to mum and dad's marriage rather than a new beginning.

Then your mind will replay all those tapes of the arguments you had with mum and dad. Time and again they can come back to you. Each time the horror and guilt of your part becomes ever more obvious in the downfall of your family.

Perhaps mum and dad split up when you were much younger and you couldn't understand what was going on and so you accepted the only explanation which your conscience, in all its bewilderment, ignorance and despair, could come up with. Over the years, as you have grown up, this theory has become engrained as truth. Even when you are older and more able to understand the true strains marriages undergo, lack of explanation and information from mum and dad leaves all the reasoning to your imagination.

The temptation is always there for you to blame yourself, but it is rarely justified. Everyone can look back at arguments they have caused or things they shouldn't have said or done. It is all too easy to point to these and say they were the cause, especially when mum and dad haven't told you what the real problem was. But it should take much more than a series of arguments to break up a family. There must be something else, some underlying fault.

If your birth was the final desperate attempt by mum and dad to make something of their relationship, their expectations were totally unrealistic. Babies are not romantic things when yelling and smelling at 3 o'clock in the morning! It is not you who are to blame in this situation, it is mum and dad's naivety.

Regardless of your parents' expectations you may question whether life would have been less stressful and therefore more bearable without you around. On the one hand the answer is almost certainly 'yes!' Parenthood is a highly skilled and difficult task. On occasions it is also totally exhausting and draining. But, and it is a big but, it is a task God has equipped us all for by creating us in his image, the image of a perfect parent. On the other hand, even accounting for the added strain that you might have brought to mum and dad's marriage, there must have been some underlying weakness for which you are not to blame.

Furthermore, even without you around, other stresses would have revealed these weaknesses. Perhaps the greatest of these stresses would have been the longing for the fulfilment of having you as a baby! The pursuit of a career or some other goal brings its own stresses.

So even if you consider yourself to have been

a mistake, there are no grounds for you to believe you wrecked mum and dad's marriage. Quite simply, there is no such thing as 'a mistake'. Not to God anyhow. When you were conceived he didn't look astonished and say, 'Gosh, how did that happen?' To the Creator of the universe you were a delight, a miracle, an expression of beauty and love. Now if your mum and dad didn't see it that way, that is their failing and not yours. It is most unfair to blame you for their failings. This is equally true if your conception was outside of your mum and dad's marriage and caused it.

5 Inner space: The feelings strike back

. . . what about the feelings that you just can't keep hidden?

Rejection, fear, and just feeling that it's all your fault: these are the kinds of emotions that you might be able to keep hidden from everyone else. But not all emotions are like that: what about the feelings that you just can't keep hidden? That's what this chapter is all about. . .

I'm jealous of friends whose families are still together

Struggling to come to terms with what's happened to your family is bad enough. Having to do it when you're surrounded by friends and school mates who seem to live in family bliss is like hitting a man when he's down. No wonder you can end up feeling jealous and full of self-pity. Why should they have a monopoly on all the happiness? Why don't they realise how hurt I feel? Perhaps you have to spend the summer term hearing about everyone else's up-and-coming summer holiday, knowing that your mum couldn't possible afford to take you anywhere.

In this kind of situation it's perfectly natural for you to feel twinges of jealousy. Those kind of feelings are going to be part of coming to terms with what's happened. But it's vital that you deal with them when they arise instead of having a massive pity party!

Jealousy is a very destructive emotion. It can never get us what we're jealous about. It's the kind of emotion that always leaves us worse off. Deep down, perhaps we feel that the greater fortune of others is a sign of God's greater love for them.

Nothing could be further from the truth. As

you struggle with all these feelings, God has not forgotten you. As impossible as it may sound, God's feelings of hurt and anger at what has happened to your family are even more intense than your own. Rather than denying you love, he wants to show his perfect and powerful love more than ever before.

Perfect because he didn't cause what has happened to your family. His love only wants the best for you.

Powerful because, although God doesn't always intervene in history and stop families breaking up, he can heal the very deep and painful emotions you feel right now.

How do I deal with jealousy?

1 If your friends are being particularly insensitive in talking about their families, you must be prepared to tell them how you feel. Alternatively you may find it easier to tell your closest friend and ask them to make sure that everyone understands what you're going through and becomes a bit more sensitive.

2 Be honest enough to admit that there are many other teenagers in the world who are worse off than you: some may be struggling for survival in poor countries, others may have lost their parents altogether.

3 Ask God to forgive you for begrudging your friends their own happiness and ask him to help you to deal with the way you feel.

4 Families where mum or dad have left and a single parent is left at home can still share positive and happy times together, as well as the difficul-

ties and grief. Losing a parent from home does not mean you will never be happy again.

I don't trust people anymore

I don't trust men or women much at the moment and I find it very hard to enter into close relationships because I am so afraid of being let down again and being without love – which is the most important thing to me.

You've probably heard about the great exploits of the French tightrope walker Blondin. Undeterred by such a weird name, Blondin became famous when he stretched out a wire across the top of the Niagara Falls. A huge crowd of excited spectators gathered to see him take a wheelbarrow across. Hundreds of feet below the waters crashed and swirled with the look water gives when it is rather peckish for the odd stupidly-named human. Having got the wheelbarrow across, the story goes that Blondin asked for a volunteer to sit in it on the return journey. Somebody was stupid enough to choose this precise moment to scratch their head . . . and got picked!

Be honest. Would you sit in a wheelbarrow and be taken across a tightrope by a Frenchman with a funny name? To do so, you'd either have to be incredibly stupid or the most trusting person yet to exist on Planet Earth.

OK, let's assume you're the trusting variety. Would you still do it, if, to start with, Blondin had three practice runs on a wire just above the ground, and managed to knock you off each time? ? ! (If you would, you'd better stop reading this and get hold of a copy of our other book: *Emergency Do-it-yourself Brain Surgery for the Incredibly Stupid*.)

The point is this. When we've been badly let down by the one person we thought we could depend on, suddenly it becomes a lot more difficult to trust them again. Or perhaps anyone else. The risks are too great. We might get hurt again and let down like the last time.

Battling with these feelings will probably take a great deal of time. Learning to trust again will be a gradual process. But it can happen. There are at least two areas we need to try to build our trust in.

Parents

Learning to trust the very people who seem to have let you down may seem an impossible task. Where they constantly continue to let you down again and again, you may be right to be wary about what they say. You may even have to accept that, in their imperfect state, your mum or your dad is not trustworthy.

However, it's important not to assume this. If you live with mum, she will probably be anxious to show you that she still loves you and wants to look after you. You need to give her a chance and not close yourself off to her. Mum's love for you may give her a sense of purpose and hope at a time when she is struggling with rejection by dad.

Many teenagers go on even to build a friendship again with the parent who has left. The situation may still cause you hurt. You may wish that your mum had never left home, but may still be able to build a friendship. Be open to this possibility, even if you feel you need some time before you attempt it.

Other men

I found that I stereotyped men in the same categories as men who have broken up lives and families. I know a few more blokes better now and I'm realising that not all of them are swines – or words to that effect! – some are great!

As Kirsty struggled with these feelings, she had to come to accept that it was ridiculous to put all men in the same boat as her dad. True, there are men – and women – who cannot be trusted and intentionally or otherwise hurt people. We are all bound to meet them at some time in our lives. But there are many many more who are quite different. They, like all of us, are still imperfect humans and may sometimes let you down . . . but remember you're exactly the same.

So can I guarantee that you'll never be let down again? No, I can't. But there are men who, to the best of their intentions, want to be loyal, trustworthy and dependable – millions of them. Hopefully you're reading the wise words of one right now! It may take time, but bit by bit you will discover this for yourself. For a while, you may find this impossible: being in the presence of men may make you nervous or afraid. Seeing a man fly into a temper may make you panic. But don't imagine it will stay this way. Take heart from Kirsty's story and begin to trust again.

I'm feeling angry

Anger has a lot to do with the chapter on forgiveness that follows. But whilst we're travelling through your heart we ought to stop and take a look at this emotion. It may be one of the strongest feelings you have.

You may be angry at your parents for splitting up, especially the parent who has left.

You are probably angry at any third party who has helped cause the break-up.

You may also be angry at God for letting all this happen to you and your family.

That's an awful lot of anger to be carrying around inside you. Such pent up emotion can affect you in different ways. You may find yourself becoming moody and stroppy, involved in petty arguments with friends or simply depressed.

Anger is OK. Provided it's directed at the right things and the right people. The problem is that often we get angry at the wrong things and the wrong people. Jesus is angry at world hunger and suffering – and, yes, family breakdown. You too can feel angry at the circumstances that have brought about a breakdown in your family and caused so much hurt and pain. But be careful.

The moment that anger turns in on itself and becomes bitter, things begin to go wrong. Like most negative emotions it will leave you worse off.

Little by little you have to come to terms with what has happened and empty your anger out from inside. I used to drive my mum mad by putting holes in her washing up gloves and filling them with water. It was great to watch the water

Anger is OK. Provided it's directed at the right things . . .

gradually empty out. (Well, I was only eight!) In the same way, all that anger needs to be emptied out of you. God doesn't expect it to happen overnight, but you must be serious about dealing with it.

Perhaps it isn't easy to even see how to start dealing with your anger. Maybe the following points will help to get you started. In my experience talking about how you feel with others you can trust is often the most helpful thing you can do.

1 Admit you feel angry. It may help even to write down what you feel angry about or where your anger is directed . . . mum, dad, yourself, God . . .
2 Ask God to help you deal with your feelings

of anger. This isn't just a vague hope! God does want to help and the simple act of beginning to pray will start that process.

3 Find someone to talk to about your feelings: a youth leader at church, a friend or anyone you trust.

I feel embarrassed that my family has failed

When mum or dad leave home, the feelings of failure may extend to you. It's not just your parents, your family as a whole seems to have failed. Faced at school by so many friends whose families are still together, this sense of embarrassment at your failure only increases. Alongside it you may feel the stigma of not being part of a 'normal' family. You may even be teased about it.

Perhaps the embarrassment of it all leads you to tell no one. Pretending that all is still well, you may find yourself avoiding questions about your family: what you did at the weekend, where you plan to go for a holiday. Perhaps you may weave a complicated story of lies to cover what has happened.

How do you cope with this? A few decades ago there is no doubt that things would have been a lot harder. The whole of society attached a stigma to divorce and family breakdown. It tended to be swept under the carpet or ignored except for disapproving glances. Much has changed since then and you shouldn't feel embarrassed at what has happened. On a purely statistical level, family breakdown is not 'abnormal', it happens to 150,000 families in Britain every year.

Your friends may be far more sympathetic than you give them credit for; their own embarrassment may be because they are unsure of how to help you. Often they find it difficult to know whether to talk to you about what has happened or never to mention it. You may need to help them know which is best. Anyone who makes fun of your situation should be ignored or, in serious circumstances, reported to school staff.

In your own heart try to begin to accept that it is not you who has failed. Feelings of fault are very common in the midst of family breakdown and deserve a section to themselves.

Where is God in all this?

When all of your life seems to fall apart, it's natural to turn round and want to fire some questions at God. After all, he is the one person who was supposed to be in control of everything. You may blame him for letting it all happen. Why didn't he stop the break-up of mum and dad's marriage and prevent all the heartache and pain that has followed? Christians believe God hears and answers our prayers, so why hasn't he heard or answered yours? Worse still, mum or dad or both may have been Christians. Why didn't their faith help them more than it did?

Aside from the question of blame, you, like many others, may find a new struggle in your understanding of God as a Father. 'Father' is no longer a positive word. For you it is linked with the rejection and hurt caused by your own dad.

Was it God's fault?

No, is the short answer. Behind that one word lies a whole host of difficult ideas and beliefs that would keep a theologian happy for the rest of his life. However we need to stress several points. First, God has restrained his involvement in the world in order to give you and me freedom of choice. He has given us responsibility for the world he has made. His laws make clear what he would like our choices to be, but they are still our choices. Wars, murder, accidents and family breakdown take place without a lightening bolt from heaven to stop them. Hands lifted in anger to strike someone do not turn to blancmange to stop hurt.

Second, that doesn't mean God leaves us to it and sits back in a celestial armchair to watch the show. We can ask God to help us, to stop wars, prevent murders and accidents and solve the problems of family breakdown. His involvement in history has almost certainly helped all of these things. But it depends on hundreds of different factors. How many parties involved are open to his help and power? How much of events are part of the spiritual battle which the Bible talks about between good and evil? How much does the strength of our prayers depend on the state of our relationship with God? It is much more likely that God can help you when you are open to him and willing for him to make a difference.

Third, whatever the question of fault, God does not sit dispassionate and removed from your hurt. The intensity and power of his love for you means that he feels your pain and suffering even more than you do. Each time you cry, he also sheds tears. Like a perfect parent he longs to pick you up in his arms and provide you with all the comfort and security that you ache for. Rather than shutting him out in this time of crisis, he wants you to open yourself up to him more than ever before.

Perhaps more than anything else, he understands something of what you feel. He even understands your feelings of anger and confusion directed at him.

The rejection you now feel Jesus felt when the very people who had proclaimed him the Messiah called for his death. The hurt you now feel Jesus felt when his friends ran away and deserted him at the time he needed them most. The desolation you feel at the loss of your dad Jesus felt when he was separated from his Father as he slowly died on the cross.

When you begin to pray and talk to God, you can be sure that he really does understand how you feel in a way that the greatest friend or counsellor could not.

Seeing God as a father

I used to find it difficult to relate to God as Father, not having a father at home after the age of eight. After chatting and praying at a Christian camp, I came to accept God as my Father. From that day the words in Luke 3:22 – 'This is my Beloved Son with whom I am well pleased' – meant a lot to me. Realising God was my Father was great!

Simon's struggle is a common one. It's hard to imagine a good father if the only one you've known is, in your eyes, anything but. Nevertheless, God is a perfect Father. Somehow in your mind you need to begin to separate your experience of your dad or mum from your understanding of God. Chapter 2 should be your starting point to understand God and his definition of fatherhood and motherhood.

Don't be discouraged if your struggle with this question is not sorted out overnight. But don't give up either. God is not waiting impatiently for you to sort out your feelings. He is ready to help you get through them.

We're almost at the end of our roller-coaster trip through your heart. Heading back however, we come across the greatest block of all: forgiveness. This one needs a chapter to itself.

6 Forgiveness and making a stand

Two boys stand in the corner of the junior school playground with the teacher towering over them both.

John had always liked his dad. In fact he had probably loved him. The only doubt about it all was that, to be honest, he had never given it much thought. Dad had just been there: a bit like Sir Roderick. You didn't think about how much you loved them till they went. Or until they let you down.

But how did he feel now? He still wanted to love his dad. He wasn't sure though whether he ought to or not. After all the hurt dad had caused, perhaps he shouldn't. But he couldn't bring himself overnight to hate someone he had always, he supposed, loved. But nor could he bring himself to love him any more either. Dad had hurt him just too much and too often.

First there was the time when dad had told him he was leaving. It was unreal. John supposed that was the biggest blow because he wasn't prepared for it. In the time it took for dad to mutter that one sentence in his bedroom doorway his life had gone from normality to chaos. Well in fact it hadn't. There followed two weird weeks when everyone knew what was going to happen but tried to pretend they didn't. Then it did.

Now that really hurt. It was horrible; mum was hysterical; dad was a fumbling, almost pitiful wreck. James was lost beneath his headphones and a *Blood Red Sky* with U2. Sir Roderick was totally bemused until finally he decided excitement like that could only mean walk time. Then he began clinging onto anyone nearby with his front legs whilst walking on his rear ones. At one stage dad was walking out, mum was clinging to him and Sir Roderick to her. It would have been more fitting if James had had the Conga on his walkman!

Again and again dad hurt him. He had waited forty-five minutes in McDonalds for dad to turn up. Within five minutes he knew he had made a mistake. It seemed the whole of his social circle had chosen that afternoon to visit McDonalds. Each wanting to know why John was sitting alone munching his way through a whole herd of beefburgers.

Finally dad had turned up but his apologetic expression said it all. It was a look which said, 'I'm sorry I'm late son, and you're probably going to wish I'd never come at all.'

What followed, John now rated as his most embarrassing moment ever. He started off cool enough but by mid-sentence had reached boiling point.

'Dad you haven't brought her with you? Dad? Oh Dad?'

Oh no, he was losing control and he couldn't stop. Already all other conversation had stopped and his friends were staring at him, mouths opened. They looked stupid but nowhere near as idiotic as he was going to.

'You promised you wouldn't. You promised, Dad, you promised!'

He was standing up and shouting now. Oh heck. This sort of thing only happens at the end of a Neighbours episode. It was as though he was watching himself perform. He desperately wanted to sit down and shut up but just couldn't. He saw himself run in slow motion to the door, and turn one last time to look at his dad's guilty face. He saw himself slowly turn back unaware of the person in the door and too late to avoid ending nose to nose with them. It took a while to identify the nostrils he was in danger of being sucked up into. Then the true horror of the situation sunk home. It was her.

At that moment the tape sped up. John pushed forward in panic and ran. He ran and ran and ran.

All the time he cried out, 'You promised, Dad, you promised.'

School the next day was a nightmare. No one said anything. No one needed to. They just looked. He would never forgive his dad. Perhaps he should, but he never could.

Two boys stand in the corner of the junior school playground with the teacher towering over them both. One child has a red tear-stained face and a slightly swollen left eye, the other has a look of contempt and stubbornness and fists clenched. The inevitable words come from the teacher's lips; 'Now Jason tell Peter you're sorry.'

Isn't it strange that from a very young age when things go wrong, we are taught to say sorry but are rarely taught to forgive others? In the third chapter we took a look at how sometimes families go wrong or even break up: what is our reaction when this happens? Do we reckon that our dad should say sorry? Do we go out of our way to make him feel sorry? Do we blame the woman that took our father away and does this blame turn to bitterness and anger?

When either dad leaves home or mum decides to move in with someone else there will be a reaction in us. If we love our parents there has to be. This may be anger, rejection, hate, confusion, disappointment, even a sense of guilt. As the weeks, months and years go by some of these feelings do not go away. Some settle down into resentment and bitterness. This happens particularly when your parents constantly let you down or break promises, or when you see other families apparently together and enjoying life.

How do we react in the face of our family breaking up? Do we stand up to the person we feel is in the wrong? Can we forgive and forget what that person has done – or both?

Standing up for what is right

If someone you love does something you feel is wrong and it hurts you a lot, what do you do? Can you just say, 'Oh, it doesn't matter and I forgive you anyway!' You may think that would be the Christian thing to say. But I'm not sure.

If we really do love that person we should be prepared to face them and tell them that we disagree with what they are doing and even think what they are doing is wrong. Jesus often stood up for what was just and true, as he saw people being mistreated and abused.

So when you are faced with mum leaving home, or if she has already left home, you need, in a loving way, to tell her what you are feeling. That you think what she is doing is wrong and hurtful, to you, your dad and the rest of the family. Now she may not listen or do anything about it. But at least you have confronted her and told her that you feel what she is doing is wrong.

Having stood up against what you think is wrong, what do you do next?

Not holding a grudge

'I'll never forgive him for what he has done!'

Have you ever said that to someone? When someone has hurt you deeply this might be quite a natural reaction. It is difficult for any of us to be hurt without feeling angry and hitting back. But Christians cannot just leave it there, as I said earlier in the chapter on feelings and anger.

One of the most important questions you have to ask yourself is, 'Can I forgive?' Your immediate response may be, 'No!'

'How can I forgive my dad for what he did to me?'

'How can I forgive my mum for finding another boyfriend?'

'Do you expect me to forgive the woman who "stole" my father?'

This may sound too much to ask but I think that's what God wants us to do.

To forgive someone is not to say that what they have done is right or doesn't matter. Instead it means to admit that it was wrong, it hurt you, but that you are prepared not to bear a grudge against that person.

I will try to explain why I believe you should forgive others who have hurt you.

Why forgive?

Because God has forgiven you

There are many hard things Jesus asks us to do as we follow him. One of these is to forgive. One of the most mind-blowing statements that Jesus ever made was, 'For if you forgive men when they sin against you, your heavenly Father will also forgive you. But if you do not forgive men their sins, your Father will not forgive your sins.'

Once Peter, one of Jesus' disciples, was obviously upset with somebody and he asked Jesus, 'How many times shall I forgive my brother when he sins against me? Up to seven times?' You can almost hear in his voice the fact that he thinks that forgiving someone seven times would be more than enough. After that you have every right to whack them in the face!

Jesus' reply to Peter's question must have left him dumbfounded: 'I tell you not seven times, but seventy times seven.' By this I don't think Jesus meant $70 \times 7 = 490$. So we should forgive people 490 times and then . . . whack them in the face! But rather if we keep on forgiving someone by the time we reach the 200th time we may have got into the habit of being a forgiving person just as God our Father is forgiving.

Jesus then goes on to tell the well-known story of the unforgiving servant, who owed loads of money to his master. When he was called on to repay his debt, because he had no money, he pleaded for mercy from the master, who felt sorry for his servant and forgave him the whole debt.

So far so good! But now the story turns sour. The servant left the master and came across a friend of his who owed him a few pounds. He grabbed the man by the throat and demanded to be repaid! The poor guy also had no money so pleaded for mercy. Unmoved by his pleading the servant threw his friend into prison.

When all this got back to the master he called his servant in and gave him an earful. 'You wicked servant! I forgave you all that debt of yours because you begged me to. Shouldn't you have had mercy on your fellow servant just as I had on you?'

As Jesus finished the story he was quick to

draw the analogy between the master and God, and us and the servant. He explained that if God has forgiven us so much, we can do the same for others.

You have to admit it makes sense. Paul, the famous missionary, summed it up this way: 'Bear with each other and forgive whatever grievances you may have against one another. Forgive as the Lord forgave you.'

As you realise how much God has forgiven you in the past, could you start to forgive your mum, dad or step-parent?

It is good for you
From time to time I see things on the TV that stay fixed in my mind for along while. One such time was a couple of years ago when in the same week I saw two interviews. One was with the father of a woman killed in an IRA bomb attack in Enniskillen and the other was with the parents of one of the victims of a vicious murder.

The contrast between them was amazing.

The father of the bomb victim told how he forgave the murderers of his daughter, while he admitted what they had done was an outrage. He seemed on the interview to have a peace and contentment with life which I really admired.

What a contrast to the other parents who, twenty years after their child had been savagely murdered, longed to wreak revenge on their daughter's murderess. They appeared bitter and twisted. Not only had they been robbed of their daughter's life, but they had missed out on living life themselves. For twenty years their lives had been dominated by unforgiveness and the desire of getting their own back. It's amazing what bearing a grudge can do to you.

So not forgiving your mum or dad, or any one else for that matter, can seriously damage your health! Not physically, perhaps, but certainly in your emotions. You could easily become bitter and resentful. This may lead to you becoming hard and uncaring.

Bearing a grudge and not forgiving someone probably won't hurt them. You may think that not forgiving mum or dad is a way of getting back at them but it tends to turn in on itself and hurts you more. It can become like a prison to us and only with Jesus' help can we forgive and be set free. When you have done this you will be released from the hurt and you can start to care again.

You can't change the past, so do yourself a favour and save yourself a lot of misery. Why not try to forgive the people who have hurt you most and enjoy the future?

How do I forgive?

'Impossible!'

'I've tried to but I can't.'

'I don't feel I can forgive.'

These may be some of your reactions to the thought of forgiving the one you feel is the guilty party in your family breakdown. It is a hard thing to do but let's take it step by step.

They don't deserve to be forgiven

This is most people's initial thought. In fact what they have done may be awful and hurtful. The results of their actions may constantly be on your mind. But this does not alter the facts. God has forgiven you some awful things even though you didn't deserve it. Not only that but bearing a grudge only hurts us more in the end.

I don't feel I can forgive

This is the next hurdle to overcome. We think we must feel something to be able to forgive. We think we need to love someone before we can forgive them. It seems impossible after all they have done? Well it isn't true. Forgiveness is not a feeling, it is a decision. It is an act of your will. You make up your mind to forgive and that's it. But don't panic, read on!

This is the next hurdle to overcome.

Even then it is still very hard to forgive, however important it might be. When you've been badly let down you might not feel strong enough to forgive, however determined you are. But remember what we've already said about God's love. He loves you totally and will never let you down. The more you know this love personally, the less difficult it is to forgive. It will never become easy though!

I'm not sure I want to forgive
The next step has to be that you are willing to forgive. Some people say that they would like to be able to forgive but they just can't. If you feel like this, you need to pray, perhaps with another person. Ask God to make you willing to forgive. It may take a while to get to the stage where you can honestly say that you don't hold a grudge against that person. Other things they have done may keep on coming into your mind. Each time this happens try to forgive them. It may not be easy but it's the only way to get free from the hurt of the situation.

I'm not sure what I need to do to forgive
To forgive someone you don't necessarily need to see them. You could pray and tell God that you are prepared not to hold a grudge anymore. You may feel you need to write a letter to the person who has hurt you telling them that you have forgiven them. It may take a while for you to get to the place where you can forgive. But give it a chance.

Take things step by step and don't imagine that you can sort through everything overnight. It can help to think about what your feelings are towards dad and mum: these may include anger, hate, love, bitterness, disappointment (and many others!). Have you been able to talk to them about how you feel? If you haven't, it's often a good idea to let them know some of the things you are feeling inside.

When it comes to beginning the process of forgiving the people who've hurt you, try thinking of the person who's hurt you most; it could be your mum, dad, mum's boyfriend, dad's girlfriend or anyone else on the scene. If you haven't been able to forgive them yet, don't panic, the first big step is wanting to be able to forgive them.

Firstly, ask God to show you how much he loves you. This may take some time but it is the most important part. Then ask him to give you love for the person who has hurt you. Remember – if God asks you to do something, he doesn't expect you to get there on your own strength. When you feel able, pray and tell God you are prepared not to hold a grudge against the person who has hurt you and tell him you forgive them. You may need to tell the person you forgive them too. You could write them a letter or tell them over the telephone. If you see them regularly, perhaps you could tell them face to face. Ask God to give you the right words to say – so that they know what you mean.

There's no prize for sorting out these relationships in the fastest possible time. As we said before, it's often a gradual process.

7 What do I do now?

When mum or dad leave home many problems you
hadn't thought about crop up.

To be honest when dad finally left home John was relieved. It had become unbearable. Now they could rebuild. But he soon realised he was wrong. Just how wrong was to become apparent not only to him but also to Sir Roderick. The hassles were only just beginning.

First of all money was tight. It didn't help that James carried on life in his typical selfish way. 'Mum, can I have some money for this? Can I have some money for that?' James knew that she didn't have any to give away. But he probably knew she felt guilty that she had caused him so much upset and so thought she ought to give it to him. Not that he ever showed any particular gratitude. James seemed like the typical brother to John.

Then things began to get nasty. John blamed Dad's girlfriend for the trouble. He had never met her but reading between the lines and judging by the influence she had had on dad so far, she was a nasty piece of work. Now dad was becoming unreasonable. First he wanted the house sold and split two ways. He wanted this done immediately. This was of course ridiculous but still upset mum. She hoped he would come back and each request like this was just another nail in the coffin of her marriage.

The requests became more and more stupid. He would ring up demanding handkerchiefs. John did wonder whether he was cracking up. Then came the last straw. Celia's kids (his girlfriend's children) were homesick. It might help if they had a dog and so he was coming round for Sir Roderick!

The house went on full alert. Even James was moved to action. A twenty-four hour minder was assigned to Sir Roderick and an elaborate invasion warning system introduced. Unfortunately it was all to no avail. Sir Roderick himself seemed for once in his life to misread the crisis of the moment and when the canine kidnapping took place it was something of an anti-climax.

Dad arrived as they were eating their meal. The door opened and just for a minute everyone was stunned. All that is except Sir Roderick who gave him his usual hero's welcome. He then contentedly waddled out down the path and stepped into the car as though he was off to the park. They were stunned not so much by the suddenness of events as the blatant disloyalty of Sir Roderick. He didn't even say goodbye.

What the threats over the house failed to do, the abduction of Sir Roderick succeeded in. Mum was moved to see a solicitor. It may not have been the first solicitor instructed on behalf of a dog. But he was somewhat bemused by a story which paid only passing reference to the breakup of a family, money troubles and threats over the house as a prelude to the main grievance – the abduction of Sir Roderick.

To cut a long story short, Sir Roderick returned a few days later. It appeared Celia's kids found him boring and wanted a real dog! A real dog indeed, thought John. He looked down at Sir Roderick as his mouth, legs and stomach began to quiver in some contented dream in front of the gas fire. This was a dog among dogs. John stroked his back affectionately. Sir Roderick jumped in terror and stood hiding with his head behind the sofa and his body blocking the lounge door. This was indeed a dog among dogs.

When mum or dad leave home many problems you hadn't thought about crop up. Some young people find themselves caught up in the midst of it all. Others are bypassed by mum and dad, but wish they had a better idea of what was going on. This chapter looks at the law and the steps that mum or dad need to take to look after home, family and even the dog. Some questions will be more relevant than others so you may like to pick and choose your way through.

Now dad has left home where could this all end?

There are three main possibilities. There could be a formal divorce, an informal separation or else dad could still come back. It is surprising how many marriages are rebuilt after a short or even long separation. It's not easy, though, as the last chapter describes.

What is divorce?

Divorce is a formal ending of a marriage on one of five grounds. The most common are adultery and unreasonable behaviour. But mere separation for two years if both parties agree, and five years if they don't, is enough for a court to grant a divorce decree. Also if mum or dad has abandoned the family for two years that is also sufficient grounds for a divorce.

But plans are afoot to change the law. In the future it is possible that either mum or dad may see a solicitor and complete a statement of marriage breakdown. This says simply their marriage isn't working. Then twelve months later the divorce will be formalised. In the meantime all the arrangements are made about you, the home, money and the like.

How are all the practical arrangements worked out?

The most stressful part of the whole process involves sorting out what happens to the family. Most of the time these arrangements are agreed between mum and dad themselves. The courts prefer it this way and will obviously abide by what mum and dad have agreed most of the time. Normally it is only when mum and dad can't agree, for whatever reason, that the courts will get involved and decide for mum and dad.

Obviously these decisions are very hard to make. But there are people and groups who exist especially to help in these situations, such as the Family Mediators' Association. You will find their addresses at the back of the book.

What happens to me?

Normally this is worked out by mum and dad, hopefully in consultation with you. In this case whoever files the petition of separation will need to set out the present and future intentions agreed between mum and dad for you. These should include where you will live and how and when you should see your other parent.

The court is most of all concerned to make sure what is agreed is the best for you. It will not get involved unless your welfare is at stake or if mum and dad can't agree.

If the court has to get involved it will make 'Orders'. These include 'Residence Orders' to decide where you should live, 'Contact Orders' to decide how and when you should meet or be in touch with the mum or dad you aren't living with and, finally, other 'Specific Issue Orders' to decide things like which school you should go to, any health issue or even, believe it or not, religion!

Again the courts will only get involved if they have to and then their sole concern is your welfare. This means your views are important even if the final decision isn't yours. A Court Welfare Officer is appointed to listen to everyone's views, particularly yours, and present a report back to the court.

This means you should be able to see both mum and dad if you want to. It also gives you a say in where you want to live.

Finally it is worth saying that if things don't work out where you're living and you are unhappy, the other parent can try to get the court's decision changed later by applying for one of the Court Orders. In fact anyone with a real interest in you, such as a grandparent, can apply if the courts will allow them.

What about the home?
The home is nearly always left for the use of the parent who has the children. A court will also usually prevent a sale of a house until all the children have finished school. If the court is unhappy about interference in the home by the other parent, it may even order the transfer of the ownership of the house into the sole name of mum or dad looking after you.

A more difficult situation arises when debts have amassed and the building society or bank want to sell the house. Officially they can. However they are normally understanding if the situation is talked through with them early enough.

What about money?

There are two problems which cause debt. One is the immediate problem as soon as mum or dad leaves home. The other is the long term problem of what, if anything, mum or dad agree to pay the rest of the family left at home, and whether they in fact do!

As soon as dad, or indeed mum, leaves home the parent who stays with you should immediately contact the Social Security office. The lower the income of your parent, the more they will be able to claim through income support, family credit and other benefits. For instance, for the first sixteen weeks the Social Security office may pay half any mortgage interest. After that they may pay all the interest. What's more, a visit to your building society or bank may result in a change of mortgage arrangements so you only make interest payments. In other words you pay out nothing on the loan itself! These visits are particularly important when, let's say, dad leaves and refuses to pay you anything!

Hopefully mum and dad can agree their intended financial arrangements amicably. But if not mum or dad needs to apply to the court, who will decide for them and seek to enforce any decision legally. The money is paid regularly, maybe weekly, maybe monthly and is called Maintenance.

Obviously there will always be situations

when, for one reason or another, you don't get the money. Once again the Social Security office will help, though it will still be tough.

This all sounds complicated – Help!

Don't panic – just take things step by step. As soon as possible you should make sure mum or dad sees a solicitor. Everything that mum or dad says to the solicitor and everything the solicitor says to them is confidential. But if mum (or dad) agrees the solicitor should be willing to answer any questions you might have yourself. Try asking. It's the solicitor's job to answer questions!

Wouldn't it be better to wait?

You might think you can't afford a solicitor, or that you don't trust them, and anyway mum or dad might come back tomorrow. All in all you wonder whether it wouldn't be better to wait a while. First of all there is something called Legal Aid which is designed to help those who couldn't otherwise afford a solicitor, so it may not cost you that much or anything at all. At least ring up a solicitor to find this much out.

Then again, not all solicitors are nasty people waiting to make a lot of money out of your misery. At least the one we met wasn't. He was a nice guy with two nice kids and a dog who was such a pansy he ran away from my pathetic excuse for a canine, Bignose! He belongs to a group called the Solicitors' Family Law Association. These are people who understand the traumas of marriage breakdown and promise to act sensitively.

In other words they won't put mum or dad off

ever coming home. They might even be able to encourage a reconciliation if that is what they want. Basically they won't force the issue and will act on his instructions as long as they aren't vindictive. They will try to keep everything as friendly as possible.

You will need advice from an early stage and a solicitor like this will help. The address and telephone number of the Solicitors' Family Law Association are at the back of this book.

Dad hasn't left home totally and he is getting really dangerous

If this is the case you need to know what you can do. The courts have powers to grant Orders either getting dad, or very occasionally mum, out of the house or else stopping him being violent to you. They have a power of arrest if these orders are broken. You will need to talk to a solicitor to apply for one.

One parent can also get an Emergency Residence order . . .

One parent can also get an Emergency Residence order if you or your brothers or sisters are being abused or abducted by the other partner. This is rare but is a safety measure until the Welfare Officer presents his report to the Court concerning your long term residence.

What about my possessions?
You may be wanting to ask whether dad or mum might take them or sell them. The answer is *no*. Of course it might be hard to stop them, but what is yours is yours and they should not be able to remove them. There is a real problem, though, over family pets. Dad may go off with the dog and it is very hard in this case to work out who the poor beast belongs to. It is no good asking him either! He will probably be happiest with who feeds him most. Sadly these sorts of arguments can often be the most fierce but obviously they aren't always the sort of thing courts particularly want to know about.

Does it have to end in divorce?
No. Mum and dad can call a halt and the family come back together again at any stage up to the final divorce. After this point mum and dad have to go right back to square one and marry again. You could then end up being a bridesmaid to your own mum and dad!

Is there any alternative to divorce?
Some people obviously disagree with divorce in principle but need the legal protection of arrangements and remedies without all the court action. There is in fact something called Judicial Separ-

ation which is just this. Your solicitor will organise it just like a normal divorce with all arrangements for home, family and money. But it won't actually be a divorce. It therefore means that your mum or your dad can't marry someone else. But Judicial Separation is useful for those who don't agree with divorce on principle and wouldn't want to remarry anyway.

You may have other questions about your particular situation which we haven't touched. If you turn to pages 115–6 you'll find a list of addresses of groups all there to help and give advice.

8 How to stay sane when your family's cracking up

. . . can leave you open to hurt and forever in limbo.

Sir Roderick's triumphal return allowed him just a few more liberties than usual. The settee was now his domain and no one seemed to have the heart to tip him off. His status was very definitely VIP (Very Important Pet!) and he was making the most of it whilst being careful to maintain his front of stupidity. This meant pretending he hadn't noticed that anything was different. In fact, as far as he could remember he had always been allowed on the settee!

However two weeks later everything changed. John was particularly fed up that night as he walked up the garden path towards the front door. He did notice a movement in the bush to his left but that wasn't unusual. Next door's cat had adopted that bush for functions best not gone into. There was a rather strange crunching sound now coming from the bush. But that had to be Aristotle himself. After all, who else would be interested in what was in that bush? Who else apart from. . . ?

The true horror of the situation came home to John as the front paws knocked him down. The rear paws landed on his brand new *Top Man* shirt and he felt the muddy damp seep through it at about the same time as he felt the tongue slime its way over his face like a mutant slug.

That was it. THAT was it. Sir Roderick was for it. There was to be no mercy. No cute legs in the air could appease him. No chasing tails round trees could humour him. The dog would get it. Not that it was entirely the dog's fault for all of John's mood. But just at this precise moment he wasn't interested in animal rights. He had steam to let off as Sir Roderick was about to discover.

He'd gone out in a bad mood. He didn't think he

was going to be able to go. Mum was upset again and he felt awful about leaving her. But he wasn't being much help there either. He had ended up shouting at her that dad wasn't coming back so she must pull herself together. Why did mum always cry to him? Why not James? I'll tell you why. James is never in, that's why. He couldn't care less. All James thinks about is James.

That final thought burst the dam of his emotions and with a yell he swung his right arm in an arc through the air space his instinct told him was occupied by a smelly-breathed canine. He prided himself on his instinct in situations like this. It rarely failed. But as his hand completed the full arc unobstructed and collided at speed with the concrete path he remembered that this was 'one of those evenings'.

He continued the yell he had begun at the outset of his hand's trip through space, but now a semi-tone or two higher and with mouth open rather than teeth clenched. He did so in time to feel the mutant slug slime up over his chin and flick into his mouth. His last thought before crying was just how chewy slugs must be.

This chapter seeks to answer some very practical questions about home, mum, dad, brothers and sisters. Every situation is so incredibly different it is hard to give general answers. Some questions won't be relevant to you. Others will be. So you may be tempted to miss out some and give yourself longer to read through the others. Alternatively, you may at this stage want to read the gripping final episode in the life and times of Sir Roderick and leave all this for another night!

Is it silly to hope the family will come back together?

No, some families do come back together even after very serious breakdowns. This is not the end of the crisis as a later chapter will explain. But don't give up hope too easily. Often a split reveals a few home truths! It might make apparent how much mum and dad do miss each other. It might also reveal the truth about other people who up to this point have seemed so attractive to either mum or dad!

However the truth must also be faced that marriages which split don't normally come back together. To hope against all the odds in the end can leave you open to hurt and for ever in limbo, unable to get on with your life fully. Hope, but don't let your hopes cloud the reality of the situation.

How do I comfort mum?

Sometimes the most distressing and difficult consequence of a family breakup is the effect it has on an innocent parent. Let's take mum for example. She suddenly finds out dad has been unfaithful. It comes as a numbing shock. For a while she is scared to confront him and lives in limbo trying to carry on as normal. In fact her whole confidence and trust has been betrayed. Finally she confronts him and hears the truth. She is to be abandoned. Her emotions run riot with feelings of rejection, failure, fear perhaps even guilt over hurting and failing you. She needs to make decisions but can't. She must keep the home running but her emotions have drained her energy.

Her response to you as her child will vary. Some mums try to put on a brave face and cover up in front of their children. In this case you may wish she would let you help her more. Others break down and their children, or perhaps one of them, are left supporting their mum. In this case it might all just be too much for you.

In the first case the frustration is that obviously you want to know what's going on. Seeing mum upset and not knowing what's happening makes it impossible to do anything about it. You are left upset with no light at the end of the tunnel and no part to play to relieve the agony.

The other scenario can be just as awful. Being able to comfort mum for a while is OK. But there comes a time when you have said all the comforting words that can be said and now they have lost their impact. You live in fear of hearing mum cry because you have nothing left to give her. You can't just leave her to cry but have run out of energy or answers to help her. You find yourself getting frustrated and angry. The horrible thing is that you even end up taking it out on mum by snapping at her.

Some children just can't cope and try and keep out of the way. This doesn't mean they don't care. It just means they are at a loss to know what to do. In fact you may be like this. Younger brothers or sisters might especially feel this way. But older ones can do too. This might leave one child to do all the comforting, which can cause them further frustration and anger.

It is important you don't take on more of a burden than you can cope with. In the end it won't do anyone any good. You need to encourage mum to share things with you, but need to realise that you probably can't bear the load on your own. You will need someone else or preferably a small group of friends. They of course have their own lives to lead and can't be there all the time. So, much of the pressure of seeing mum upset and being the only help will still fall to you.

After a while you would have voiced all the comforting words you can muster. At this stage it is perhaps best not just to keep going over and over the same ground. Rather the most comforting thing you can do is simply to show love. This might be in little ways like buying mum flowers or else just by being there to hug her. You may have no words to say but in the silence your mere presence can be comforting. Your love will help mum know a security after being so let down. It will remind her of something positive to live for. It will encourage her that her family hasn't totally fallen apart.

But what if I can't cope

It's no good trying to be stronger than you are. Everyone needs help when something as important as their family falls apart. No one is so strong that they can cope on their own with all the strains and heartbreak around them. You are no exception. You might feel like crying your heart out. You will almost certainly feel furiously angry in some way or other. You will get fed up, wondering where it will all end and why it happened to you anyway. The important thing is that you admit this and allow others to help you.

Depending on God

First of all, God understands. An Old Testament prophet, Hosea, married a wife who was proved unfaithful again and again. Hosea went on loving her and made the point that his wife's unfaithfulness was a picture of our unfaithfulness towards God. God knows what it is like to be rejected by someone we love, because he has been rejected by us. He also knows specifically how we feel because the Bible says he made us. In fact he knows and feels our hurts even better and more than we know and feel them ourselves.

Therefore he is not a God who is unable to sympathise with our sufferings. Far from it, as a Perfect Parent he longs to love us. He cries when we cry and wants to cradle us and protect us from hurt. He hears our every cry and wants to fill us with love and power to cope. He even understands our anger and frustration we may direct at him. He wants us to be honest with him, however we feel. The writers of the Psalms were not afraid to tell God exactly how they felt, even if they felt God had been particularly unfair and unhelpful, and nor should we! However, in the Psalms we find that in time the writers came to see what was really going on. Then their attitude to God changed from despair to praise.

The tragedy is that often you will be tempted to cut God out of your troubles. You may blame God or lose faith in him. You don't tell him how you feel and just ignore him. By doing this you can miss out on seeing how God can help and strengthen you so that your despair turns to praise. It is easy to see why this happens. You are too drained physically, emotionally, mentally and spiritual to pray. You are confused, perhaps angry.

Depending on friends

It was the school trip to Canterbury which brought it all out into the open. Jackie was given a form for her parents to sign and suddenly it was all too much. Right there, in the middle of the classroom, tears began to roll down her cheeks as she looked at the space on the form where two months ago, mum and dad would have both put their signatures. Quickly she brushed the tears aside and looked nervously at Emma and Sarah sitting next to her. Their looks said it all. Yes they had seen the tears. Perhaps it was time to tell them what was going on.

Sitting in the changing room at break, Jackie poured out the whole story. She'd wanted to tell them for ages but somehow, stupidly, she'd imagined they'd just laugh or not understand what it was like. Instead they listened and promised to help. As the bell went for the next lesson, Jackie felt a sense of relief. At last it wasn't just her own private nightmare, now there was someone else to face it all with her. . .

It is vital that you find some people outside of the situation on whom you can lean. You will need Christian friends who can pray for you and with you. You will need friends with whom you can unburden your problems and on whom you can cry if need be. You need friends you can trust. One of your first prayers should be for friends like this.

It may be hard at first to work out just how much to tell. What if the family were to come back together? Wouldn't it be better if no one knew what had happened? What if mum and dad have specifically asked you not to tell people what has happened? What if you don't want your mum and dad's failings to become known? For you to be able to cope, you will need help. Then you can be of some help to mum, dad and others. So it is best to tell someone or a small group of people so that they can help you. You needn't make an announcement on the *News at Ten*!

Finding the people to tell may not be easy. You probably have never been through such a big crisis before so have never had to rely on others to such a large degree either. Also, getting mum or dad to find people to turn to will be hard. You will feel guilty about putting upon other people. But this is a crisis situation and you need not feel guilty.

Depending on family

The other people you can turn to obviously include your own family. Amazingly, despite all the hurt and arguments of a family breakdown, often a crisis can bring the remainder of the family far closer together. It can be hard though at home when you want to be strong and support the rest of the family and yet feel like crying at the same time. You will need to release your feelings some- where, which is why it is important to turn to others outside the family who aren't depending on you, in this instance, to be strong. This will give you more strength to go on at home. But even then it is important to be honest with one another about how you feel even if you've talked to someone else about these emotions. Talking with your family can bring you all much closer and help the healing process.

Remember, finding yourself in a position in which you can't cope is a frightening situation. But it is here we can discover the real depths of God's love and power as well as real friendship and family.

But will my life ever be normal again?
The first days after a family has broken can be traumatic, but then sometimes the trauma seems to go on and on. If you are older and dad, let's say, is depending heavily on you, you may have a guilty conscience every time you want to go out or away. You may find yourself getting frustrated that you can't lead your own life because you are too busy propping up others. You might not feel happy bringing friends home. You might envy friends the freedom you once knew. You may wonder what on earth the future holds for you.

The answer to this one is hard. Time does heal, even though at the moment this may seem impossible. But for that healing to work there will need to be some pain. It may be that you will need to spend a lot of time in the immediate aftermath of the crisis at home, rather than doing what you would normally prefer. But life can't continue like this forever. Therefore, little by little, your lives must be allowed to return to as much normality as possible. Obviously this requires sensitivity and it will be difficult, even painful, at first. But there is something secure about normality and your normality might encourage the others to continue living their lives again which aids the whole healing process.

Sometimes this is so very hard. Others in their distress or unreasonableness might make excessive demands on you. You may even feel very guilty about going out to enjoy yourself, leaving others alone at home to their grief. But (at the risk of repeating myself) to be of any help you must be coping and sane yourself. Also, too much attention might slow the healing process. You may even find that everyone copes better than you thought without you around!

Nowhere is all this more true than in the area of school work. Comforting your family may be a good excuse for taking a break from your homework and your teachers should understand. But there comes a point where working will need to take preference over comforting, even if it means going elsewhere to do that work! Finding the right balance in all these things is extremely hard and again it is vital we have friends around to help us decide what to do.

Should I spend my own money or give it to mum?

David had worked hard every Saturday and had saved up a tidy sum in his *Cardcash* account. The summer lay ahead of him and he allowed himself to dream of holidays with friends by the sea. But other thoughts also came into his mind. How could he cheer mum up? The day to day grind of coping on her own was wearing her down. True, she was going to get away for a while to visit her sister, but what more could he do? A thought struck him and as soon as mum stepped out of the door he sprang into action.

When mum came home a few days later and collapsed tired into the armchair she had a weird sensation, not everything was as it should be. It then hit her, *nothing* was as it should be! As she explained to the local paper, she hadn't known anything of David's plan to redecorate the living room!

Money is nearly always a really big headache when a family splits up. You may be used to being fairly well off and now you have to adjust to being poorer. You might not be able to go on trips at school because you know mum can't afford it. So don't even bother bringing the forms home. You may have a guilty conscience about spending your own money when mum so obviously needs it. Giving her some money will no doubt not only help but also encourage her. But the same advice applies here as elsewhere. For you to be of the most help you will need to be coping. This means you can't cut yourself off socially. You will benefit from spoiling yourself a little from time to time. This should also help you cope more and give more to mum.

How do I help my brother and sister?
We've already seen that your brothers and sisters may react in different ways. They may be very

helpful. They may not be able to cope and just keep out of the way. They may get very upset and need a lot of help themselves. They may get very angry and take it out on mum or dad. They may even appear to go off the rails and add to all the worries. The one thing that is for sure is they will be affected and will react somehow.

If you can all pull together and support each other that is great. But it is also quite rare. Obviously, younger children especially find a family breakdown very hard to understand. But older children may not find it easy to get emotionally involved in all the heartaches of family. This doesn't mean they don't care. They may care very deeply indeed but aren't used to expressing how they feel and don't know where to begin.

You may have a number of different reactions to your brothers and sisters. You may want to protect them rather like your mum may want to protect you. But remember first of all that your brothers and sisters will want to know something of what's going on, rather like you do. Remember too that you need help and can't bear all the strain yourself.

You may, on the other hand, get angry with your brothers and sisters because you feel they aren't pulling their weight, are being unreasonable to mum or dad or else adding to the troubles. Remember that like you they have been hurt and their reaction is a response to that hurt. It may seem sometimes that they are totally insensitive, even hurtful in their arguments and attitudes. But this doesn't mean that this is how they really feel. They may be frustrated and this is the only way they can show it.

As far as possible you will need to bear with their reaction, whatever it may be. But again remember that you can't cushion them forever from the realities of the situation. What's more it won't be helpful to do so. At some point they will need to face up to some of their responsibilities. You will need to pray for them too and show real love. Through the pain you may find you will come closer together than you ever would have imagined possible.

Should I see dad and his girlfriend?

School was over for another week. Everyone cheered at the sound of the bell. Everyone that is except for Debbie. She knew her dad was waiting for her to come round for her monthly weekend with him. It wasn't him she minded so much. It was Joyce, his new wife, she found difficult. Then there was Kevin and Jason, the little brats, who came along with her from her first marriage. She still didn't know how to react to them and had so little in common with them that each month became a boring trial to be endured and here she was going again.

Your family has probably become incredibly complex overnight and is likely to get more so! Mums, dads, stepmums, stepdads, halfbrothers, step-grandparents, not to mention uncles, nieces and even disorientated pets! It will take a while to unravel what you and they want to consider family.

. . . and even disorientated pets!

Each situation is so different that there can be no simplistic rules to follow. Your first decision is who you want to see. It is hard to cut out of your life someone who could have been so important to you. On the other hand you may find that what mum or dad has done to you has been so hurtful that you no longer feel like seeing them. What's more you may find out even if you want to see mum or dad at the outset, the meetings are so strained and false for various reasons that you do not want to go on with them.

Your decision could well be influenced by mum and dad themselves. The most upsetting scenario is that you may want to see mum or dad but they don't seem too keen on seeing you. Then the parent you live with, might not want you to see the other. They might not say as much but you may feel disloyal by visiting the mum or dad who hurt them. Then again you might not want to see them but are pressurised into doing so.

If you want to see your mum or dad and they want to see you, no one can stop you. You will need to be prepared for some very difficult situations though. For instance, it may be that you will need to see mum or dad's friend whom you blame for breaking up the family in the first place. This can be very difficult for everyone. They may resent you or be trying over-hard to please you. You may not have a clue how to react to them and in the end dread seeing your mum or dad.

You may also have a lot of travelling to do to meet mum or dad and there may be many practical difficulties. Then when you do meet, you might not know what to talk about and long to go home. Your whole time could be spent talking about your other parent and life at home and you might end up feeling like a go-between rather than a son or daughter.

Life can get so complicated that, in time, you might feel you are drifting apart and that will hurt. If only there were easy answers! But there aren't. You need to make up your own mind who you want to see. Again it is important that you cope and therefore should not be pressurised into seeing someone when it is just one extra upset too many.

Alternatively, if you want to see mum or dad, you should be allowed to. You are still their son or daughter. Dad or mum back at home may not want you to for a number of reasons. Perhaps they see it as a way of getting at the other person who has hurt them. Perhaps they are scared that you will prefer to go and live with your other parent. This might be particularly the case if they are struggling for money as they look after you all the time whilst mum or dad who have you only for a day might have more money to spoil you for that short time.

Try not to give too exaggerated an account of your time with the other parent: it might make the one you're with feel second rate.

You should still be allowed to go. You should also be allowed time just with mum or dad if you can't face their new partner and families. You are, after all, their son or daughter and they do have a responsibility to care for you. But the biggest heartache comes when it appears they don't want to know.

It may be that they do care and you are just reading the signs wrong. But then this is hardly your fault if you have already been let down badly. To you, this might appear to be the ultimate and final rejection. It might come some years later and might be a gradual drifting apart, in which case it might also bring back all the hurts you have just overcome. Many have found it helpful to write a letter to mum and dad to say you still care, can forgive them and want to stay or get back in contact. This letter then stands as an open offer. If mum or dad want to answer it they will. If not you might need once again to work through all the points in chapter four on 'overcoming hurts'.

How do I cope with step-parents?

If losing a parent isn't bad enough, gaining a new one can be horrendously unsettling. The worst scenario is if the step-parent that moves in is the one you blame for causing all the upset in the first place. But any new stepmum or dad can be unsettling. Even the budding of a new relationship has its weird aspects. You might find yourself sitting in front of the telly while mum gets ready to go out on her latest date. You kiss her goodbye and tell her not to be late in, all the time wondering whether you might not have got your roles mixed up a little!

Again each situation is so different. Some step-parents come as a real relief. They bring back a stability and happiness to mum or dad which in turn takes a load off your mind. You are therefore happy to accept them into your home. Others bring this happiness to mum or dad but most certainly not to you or your brothers and sisters. This makes you feel bad as you want mum or dad to be happy. It makes mum or dad feel bad since they might still feel guilty about hurting you before and therefore aren't prepared to do so again. It makes your potential stepmum or dad feel extremely awkward. It is a trying time for everybody!

It helps to realise how difficult everybody finds it. Being prepared to talk about things is a great help too. You may not like the guy for very good reasons. On the other hand it may be that you would resent anyone coming into your home and taking the place of your mum or dad. This might be especially the case if you feel the mum or dad who is being replaced was the 'innocent' party, the replacement was the 'guilty' party or they bring with them a ready-made packaged family of noisy obnoxious little kids! Of course, horror of horrors all three might be the case! The thought of calling this person mum or dad or indeed anything that isn't rude might just be too much to bear.

If they come, every little change they make will grate with you. If you go to live with them you will probably feel very awkward. In the end you may feel like just running away. This is where again you will need to find friends you can turn to. You can talk to them about how you feel and perhaps find a retreat to normality in them and their families. It may seem a load to put on people, but then you are a special case! God knows this and particularly wants to love and empower you to be able to cope.

There are so many other things that cause upset it is impossible to list them all. Having to move away from friends or home, even missing your own pet dog are all understandable hurts and traumas you may face. However silly or little the upsets may be, you should never feel embarrassed about telling someone you can trust about them. God cares, and if the Creator of the Universe does, so must we.

9 When mum or dad comes home

. . . finally he and mum have patched things up.

What could be better? After months of hurt and rejection since dad left, finally he and mum have patched things up. Dad, as you'd always dreamed and hoped, comes home again. Your family is back to normal at last. This doesn't happen in many cases; but if it has happened to you, read on!

If only it was this simple. Facing the prospect of seeing dad again may, in fact, fill you with dread. Can you ever trust him again after all that has happened? He may make promises that things will change but somehow they seem hollow after all the ones he's broken. Should you go on as if nothing happened? Should you expect and demand an apology for all the hurt he has caused? In the back of your mind may be the fear that one, two, even three years along the line, it will all happen again.

Coping with dad coming back home may be harder than coping when he left. Mum and you and your brothers or sisters may have settled down into a new routine. Finally you were beginning to come to terms with what had happened. Now everything has changed again. Perhaps you feel a protectiveness over mum having seen her hurt so much already. Mum and dad's relationship could still be under great strain. Tensions and arguments may still be common. Suddenly things seem even more uncertain than before. At least you knew where you stood then.

Part of the problem may be that your position changed when dad left. New responsibilities and challenges faced you. Mum depended on you to do some of the things dad would have done in the past. But now, having begun to settle into these responsibilities, everything must change again. Dad, on his return, will want to resume his position. You may have to retreat and even resent dad for coming back. These changes may create difficult tensions and are best talked through. Dad may need to realise that you have become a great deal more mature through all that has happened and begin to treat you as more of an adult.

the crisis is over....
Dad is coming home!

At best dad's return home could genuinely signal the end of the crisis.

At best, dad's return home could genuinely signal the end of the crisis. The shock of separation may have challenged both your parents to make a renewed attempt at their marriage. A new readiness to give and to love may bring a welcome freshness to their relationship. Alongside this, both mum and dad may treat you with a new maturity. They may understand the need to be more honest with you. They may want to say sorry for all the hurt they have caused you. Without denying this hurt and pain, you may be ready to forgive them and renew your own relationship with them. Just as your parents kept on loving you when you let them down and disobeyed them, they may now be asking the same of you.

At worst, you may find it impossible to face the one person who has let you down more than anyone else. The hurt dad caused you and your family may be so deep that you find it unbearable even to talk to him. To have an imperfect dad at a distance was hard, to have him back in the home is a frightening prospect. To begin to trust your dad again seems a daunting task.

Where dad's readiness to change and restore his marriage is genuine, this should be your aim, however daunting. But as you move towards this, he should also be prepared to move towards you. It isn't unreasonable for you to expect him to offer some kind of explanation and heartfelt apology for the trouble he caused. If he does not, you may have to accept that your relationship with him will be tarnished until he does. In many ways it should also be dad who starts this process. If you can find the strength, even though you don't perhaps need to, the first move could come from you.

In all this, what I am really saying is give him a chance to prove his intentions. Real love necessitates the willingness to restore relationships and give a new chance. Not to forget, but to forgive.

10 Can all this be happening to me?

Sitting up there alone I was very afraid.

For some of you reading this book, the contents will frighten you. Not because you are in the midst of a family breakdown or divorce, but because you are afraid that it's about to happen in your family. Mum and dad spend the evenings arguing. Your brothers and sisters may be turning to you with their own fears and questions. Is dad going to leave home? All the signs are there and you don't know what to do to stop it.

If that's how you're feeling, this is a chapter written for you.

We have already seen the many complicated issues at play when a relationship as deep as marriage begins to be threatened. Each situation, including your own, raises different issues. So, without knowing something of your problems, it's impossible to give a simple 'yes' or 'no' to your question. Instead I can offer some basic points to help you through the maze of confused thoughts and fears you might be feeling.

Impossible but true

It's disgusting I know, but I have a friend who can eat three *Mars Bars* at once. His mouth contorts like an astronaut taking off into space, and his teeth are probably going to rot before he's twenty-five, but it's true, however impossible it sounds.

Believe it or not, it is also possible for your family to stay together, however unlikely that seems to you. For all the thousands of families that break up each year, millions more stay together. Many, many of those millions have parents that argue and fight. But they don't break up. One of my enduring memories of growing up at home is sitting upstairs in my bedroom one day, listening to my parents argue. I heard my mum shout and cry between taunting half sentences about money problems.

Sitting up there alone I was very afraid. I'd never heard anything like this before. My immediate reaction was to think that they would separate. In fact, they didn't. And looking back now. I can see some things a little clearer than I did then:

1 Arguments are part and parcel of relationships between imperfect human beings. All couples argue from time to time. Faced with financial and other pressures, this is particularly common in marriage. On occasions they could be tense and loud, but they do not necessarily signal the end of the relationship.

2 All marriages go through times of difficulty. Your parents, like anyone else, can grow apart or begin to take each other for granted. Perhaps your own experience with boyfriends or girlfriends has already illustrated this to you. Often this might signal the end of a teenage romance. Being married however, involves a deeper commitment to work through these times until things get better.

3 Picking up odd bits of conversation and arguments rarely gives you the whole picture. Don't assume that your interpretation of events is the correct one.

4 Parents do sometimes decide to spend a short time apart to sort out their feelings and problems, and then come back together again. The separation does not always mean the relationship is over.

When the worst is true

If your parents are going through a time of difficulty or crisis in their marriage, what should you do?

Don't take on the wrong challenge

It's important that you don't fall into the trap of taking on the responsibility of saving your parents' marriage yourself. It is their relationship and they must work out the answer themselves. However, you can help in other ways. The most important factor will be your attitude to them: becoming sulky and uncooperative won't help.

Don't take sides

Where possible, be careful not to take sides in arguments between your parents. It's easy to misjudge what's going on and falsely accuse one of them of being wrong. Many teenagers have made accusations and, after some time has gone by and they've reconsidered the situation, realised that they were wrong. That is not to say that we should ignore or gloss over obvious problems. Where dad has left home with new girlfriend, we know it is wrong. But not all arguments are as clear cut.

Don't confront in the midst of emotions

It's better to wait until your parents have cooled off before expressing your concerns and worries. Perhaps later on, take the chance to tell them about your fears. It's important you don't keep them bottled up inside you. Explain to your parents that you realise that every marriage goes through periods of stress and strain. You'll get much further if you explain how their arguing makes you feel rather than trying to point out where you think they're going wrong. Ask them what you can do to help ease any tensions. Honesty like this is difficult, but may well be vital in letting your parents understand they can't hide what's going on and that they need to be open with you as well.

Confide in a friend

Somewhere in the mists of time, someone wrote that 'A problem shared is a problem halved.' And you know what? They were right. The more things bottle up inside you, the more of a distorted picture you will draw of events. Panic and fear stop us from keeping things in perspective. It's good to chat with a best friend about what's going on but remember that, if they're your age, their wisdom and experience may also have it's limi-

Panic and fear stop us from keeping things in perspective.

tations. Better, possibly, to talk to your minister, youth leader or teacher. Whether or not they are able to give you clear advice, simply telling someone else about your feelings can make an enormous difference.

If you really do find yourself alone, we offer our address at the back of the book. If you need it, we'd be happy to write and encourage you.

Confide in God

Your most dependable strength and reassurance can come from God. Share with him your inner fears and hopes. Make your prayers count too. Pray for your parents: for commitment to continue under the current strain. Pray for your brothers and sisters, one by one. Pray for yourself, for wisdom and courage to deal with whatever happens.

It's hard in a book to express the strength you can find in these quiet times of talking with God. I hope you discover for yourself the sense of security and love that streams from heaven as you begin to talk with your Father God and unburden your heart. Perhaps now is the time to put down this book and start.

11 Sir Roderick . . . The final instalment

Sir Roderick stopped in his tracks . . . he stared in amazement at what he saw.

To say that life at 8 Beaconsfield Road was easy over the next months would be untrue. John, James and the rest of the family all had their times of feeling sad and depressed. Each of them would, on occasions, seek out the solitude of their bedroom and sit quietly reflecting on what had happened. Tears were common. Mum was good at putting a brave face on it. John, though not James, realised it was just that: pretending things were OK. The time he'd rushed into the kitchen from school and found her crying over the cooker had been embarrassing. It was hard to explain to James when he complained at tea of the chips being all soggy and salty.

For Sir Roderick also, life settled back to a routine. True it was Master John who accompanied him to the park each morning. In the past it had been John's dad who dangled the lead in front of him before going off to work. But Sir Roderick didn't mind who he took over there as long as they let themselves off the lead when they got to the open ground. Humans were very insecure. The moment he went off in another direction they would shout and scream his name until he turned round. The burden of looking after the whole family was certainly a heavy one but Sir Roderick took on the task with assured determination.

Perhaps it was the fact that it was John now taking Sir Roderick across to the park, and that he took a different route to his dad, that led to Sir Roderick's final and tragic downfall.

Or perhaps it was the fact that Sir Roderick was far more stupid than he looked – which was very stupid indeed.

It all started one Tuesday morning: 7.45am to be precise. John's mind was locked into the prospect of a daunting day at school. Dad had always helped him with maths. Now he was on his own and was even looked to by James for advice on things trigono-metrical. John felt the change acutely. If there was one thing John was sure of it was this: he would never himself fall in love and get married. Relationships are dangerous, painful things. Best avoided where pos-sible.

Sir Roderick, on the other hand, was just inspecting the local trees with some concern. A further sniff con-firmed it. An intruder was at large. Only a few minutes before it had left its mark right where he was standing. If he hurried, he could catch the blighter. Show them who was in charge in this neck of the woods. There was room for only one paw print round here.

'Whhhaaaaatttt! Slow down you maniac! No wait, I'll let you off the lead if you'll give me a chance.'

Freed from the restraint of pulling a human around the park, Sir Roderick went into overdrive and charged round the bend. The scent was more powerful now. He got ready to bare his teeth. Always guaranteed to frighten them when he did that. There! That was them! Dog and human in the distance. A few seconds to impact.

Sir Roderick stopped in his tracks. Frozen to the spot he stared in amazement at what he saw.

Standing in front of him, looking quite innocent, was the most beautiful, gorgeous, delightful poodle he had ever seen. Her eyes blinked and stared in apprehension. She obviously thought Sir Roderick was about to leap forward in attack. Sir Roderick, however, was having second thoughts about the whole thing. Suddenly he didn't mind so much about the infringe-ment of his territory. Perhaps there was room for two after all.

'Ah, there you are,' said John, exhausted from the chase, stumbling up to the immobile group of two dogs and one owner. And it was the owner that occupied his attention. Claire Marks was smiling at him.

'Is this your dog?'

John blushed.

'Well, sort of. He doesn't listen to us much, but we feed him, so I guess you could say we look after him.'

Sir Roderick might have questioned this, had his eyes and attention not still been firmly on the vision of beauty before him. As it was, John's comments went unnoticed.

Perhaps this was John's chance. Someone up there in heaven had ordained this meeting. Given him the opportunity finally to ask Claire out. In the back of his mind he remembered what he had been thinking of a few moments before. He thought of mum and dad, of all the pain they'd gone through. Deep in his heart was still the same fear that it could happen to him. It felt like he was standing on the top diving board of the local swimming pool, looking down at the water below.

But the past months had begun to change John. Gradually there was dawning in him an important realisation. Alongside the dangers and the risks, love also carried the greatest rewards. If he shut himself off forever, he would be the loser.

He jumped.

'Perhaps both these mutts need some training. There's a class on Monday nights at the church hall. Want to come?'

Talk of who owned who might have passed Sir Roderick by, but even the poodle facing him couldn't stop him from hearing this. Training? TRAINING! The word struck fear into the heart of every true hound. Never!

Just as he was about to turn tail and make a run for the safety of the trees, the poodle caught his eye again. She did look rather lovely.

He thought of the prospect of a weekly rendezvous with this vision of beauty. He thought of the horrors of some old lady telling him to go and pick up a smelly sock at the other end of the room. In a moment the decision was made.

'Sounds great, provided your dog wants to come. You did say he made his own decisions.'

John and Claire looked down.

Sir Roderick's tail began to wag.

IMPORTANT ADDRESSES

The authors:
Chris Curtis, Tim Dobson and Colin Piper
George Muller Foundation
Muller House
7 Cotham Park
Bristol BS6 6DA

Where your family can find help sorting out their disagreements and practical problems:
The National Family Conciliation Council
Shaftesbury Centre
Percy Street
Swindon
Wiltshire SN2 2AZ
(0793) 514055

Family Mediators' Association
The Old House
Rectory Gardens
Henbury
Bristol BS10 7AQ
(0272) 500140

Family Welfare Association
21 Kempson Road
London SW6
(071) 7362127

Relate: Marriage Guidance
Look up the branch nearest to you in the phone directory.

Where to find helpful family law solicitors and get legal advice:

Solicitors' Family Law Association
PO Box 302
Keston
Kent BR2 6EZ
(0689) 850227

Children's Legal Centre
20 Compton Terrace
London N1
(071) 3596251

Confidential helplines for young people:
(these calls are free)
Childline 0800 11 11
NSPCC 0800 800500

BIBLE REFERENCES

If you'd like to look up any of the quotes taken from the Bible here's a list for you: